EXPONENTIAL PRODUCTIVITY

Thank you for taking the time to read Exponential Productivity, where you will find out how to:

- Leverage up to a week of personal time every month to do what you want

- Manage stress, fatigue, and overwhelm more effectively

- Start living your personal best and multiply the results you love in your life

It's not only about getting more things done, but also which things and why, that will take you to the exponential levels of achievement that you desire, and lower your stress and frustration in the process.

Best wishes

Jacques

Preface

If you're anything like me, you work in an office at least some of the time, and you've probably thought about what it would be like to have a better life, whatever that means to you. It could be more income, a promotion, a career change, more family time, less stress, better health, more fun, a holiday on a tropical island, the time and inspiration to express your creativity, or start a business on the side. You consider yourself to be capable of achieving above average results, and you've already achieved some important goals in your life. You work hard at your career and value your significant relationships, but sometimes the pressure of trying to balance your work and personal life can become stressful, frustrating, demotivating, and even overwhelming when there are so many competing demands on your time. You are so busy that it has become difficult to focus your time and energy on what matters most to you. How do you feel when you look at or even think about your schedule, your inbox, or your task list? How often do you manage to spend quality time with your loved ones, without being distracted, or just too exhausted to really engage with them properly?

Are you an aspiring professional? Would you like to reach a new level of personal mastery, experience more significance in your daily life, knowing that you are making a real difference, and be appreciated and recognized for your contribution? I imagine that may be a small part of the reason why you're reading this book, and my hope for you is that it will help you to take another step towards your goal.

Table of Contents

Introduction to Exponential Productivity 8

Part 1: Leverage - My Favorite Three Simple
Productivity Tips for the Office................................20

    Chapter 1: Complete Workflow Mastery - Empty
    your Inbox...20

    Chapter 2: One Structured List - The Foundation
    for Prioritizing 28

    Chapter 3: Planning for Action – Leverage your
    Schedule..38

Part 2: Productivity with Purpose 47

    Chapter 4: New Routines to Transform Old Habits
    - A Process...47

    Chapter 5: Your Filter of Focus - The Next Level
   61

Introduction to Exponential Productivity

Most of us have heard it said that we cannot manage time, because it is a constant that cannot be manipulated. You can only manage what you do and how you do it, in the time that you have available. We all have the same 24 hours available each day, but some manage to accomplish more during that time than others, and a special few manage to accomplish exponentially more – achieving extraordinary and exceptional results! Robin Sharma often mentions world champion athletes as an example, to illustrate the difference between those who operate at world-class level, and those who are comfortable with mediocrity. World champions have a different time-table, they are focused, they have a goal and a powerful vision of the future, they get up earlier, they spend more of their time on the activities and training that will get them to where they want to be, they enlist the help of coaches and trainers, and so the list goes on. You and I may not be world-class athletes, but if we want to achieve better results or even just be more productive, we have to start doing things a bit differently to the way the average person does.

In productivity training workshops, we typically ask the question, if you were given an extra hour every day, what would you choose to do with it? It's a good question, because it gets you thinking about what is most important to you. I recently exchanged two hours of sitting in traffic congestion daily, for two hours of sitting quietly at my desk writing this book. At other times in my life I have leveraged my schedule in order to learn new skills, get into better physical shape, build a new relationship, or start new businesses.

If you can learn to better leverage *what* you do with your time, rather than just *how* you do it, you will be able to create and add so much more value - for yourself, your loved ones and your business, or your manager and your organization. The first part of this book focuses on the 'how' with my take on some basic productivity principles that you can implement immediately, and the second part focuses on answering the 'what' and the 'why' questions of productivity. By clarifying your personal values and goals, you will uncover where to spend more of your time, to create the life and results that you want. Tony Robbins said, "If you do what you've always done, you'll get what you've always gotten."

The challenge is that we all know how difficult it is to change. We live in a time where change has become a constant, and information overload is a given. There is simply more to do than time available to do it in. Your ability to grow, adapt, and prioritize effectively, has become critical not only to your success, but to your survival. A few key skills need to be mastered, so that you can focus on taking ownership of your results and really leverage your impact.

It shouldn't take longer than a couple of hours to read this book, but it should provide you with some extra momentum as you start to see the potential of what can be achieved. Here is a simple example from my daily routine that I've been implementing over the past few months.

I recently changed my daily routine to leverage a week of personal time every month to do something that was important to me. This particular example may not resonate with everyone, but I'm going to share with you how I did it, because the approach can be applied in different ways to different situations. You will be able to find your own solutions and innovations to get the results that you want. The book you're reading right now is my proof of concept, because I wrote and published it during the extra time that I leveraged.

Before I made any changes I would spend about 90 minutes in peak traffic every morning and every evening, arriving at work or home exhausted and frustrated. I was trying to get this book written and I simply wasn't finding enough time or energy to write. So I made three strategic changes to my daily schedule:

1)   I started waking up an hour earlier.

2)   I also started going to sleep an hour earlier at night, so as not to lose out on any valuable sleep.

3)   Lastly, I started leaving the office an hour later.

This enabled me to leverage two hours per day, one in the morning and one in the evening, both at times when I could work without interruptions. By missing the peak traffic hours, my commute time was drastically reduced, so I would still arrive home at the same time to have supper with my family in the evenings. I effectively exchanged two draining hours of time in the traffic for two extra quiet hours at my desk every week day.

The most important part of this story is what I decided to use the extra time for. I didn't want the extra time just to get ahead with my regular work. I wanted to finally do some writing! That was the starting point and the motivation for me to make the change in the first place. You may want to master a new skill through part-time study, or anything else that's important to you. This book was the goal that energized me and provided the extra motivation to get up at 5am. Obviously I sometimes got it wrong by sleeping in, staying up a bit too late, or using my extra office hours for other urgent tasks, but on average it was a massive win for me.

Let's look at the mathematics behind the concept:

<u>One extra week of personal time per month</u>

I normally work an 8 hour day, 5 days a week. So 2 extra hours x 5 days per week x 4 weeks in the month = 40 hours (which is equivalent to 5 x 8 hour working week days). That may seem like cheating, but you're reading the book I wrote in that time. Leveraging a week per month amounts to three months leveraged over the course of a year. It was a deliberate decision to work on this book during that time, because I knew that when I hit "Publish", I would have something tangible to show for the decision I made and the work that I put in during that time. It's not just about the time I leveraged, but also what I chose to do with that time. Being able to share the value that these principles have added to my life is important to me. It provides the opportunity to make a small difference, by connecting with others who share similar challenges.

I realize that the schedule tweaks I used to create my monthly week of personal time are not going to be practical for everyone, but the underlying idea can be applied in different ways to suit different lifestyles and situations. Even if you can only manage to recover an extra half hour per day from your schedule, where you choose to be and what you decide to do during that time could make a significant difference.

Exponential

I started 2017 with a rough draft of this book that was only about 50% complete after two years, because I just wasn't finding the time to write. By using these productivity principles, I was ready to publish within 90 days. That's an increase of 1600% in my performance. By using two key strategies:

a) I used the productivity principles to buy back time by tweaking my schedule to find an extra two hours per day to do what I wanted,

b) I prioritized what I chose to do with that time, based on the highest value tasks that were aligned to my personal priorities. This multiplied my results by x16! These are not average results. Now think about what it would be like to improve one of your key performance areas by 16 times.

The Exponential Productivity Blueprint

From the traditional business productivity formula of outputs over inputs, we can derive a simple formula for personal productivity:

Exponential Productivity Formula = Value / Time

Value (Describes your Outputs)

Your contribution or value-add in any particular area of your life. For example, in

• Your business: this could be your core offering of a product or service, measured in number of clients, number of sales, or sales value, etc.

• Your Career: this could be your key performance areas, linked to specific organizational metrics.

• Your personal life: this could be quality time activities spent in your significant relationships, on a daily, weekly, or monthly basis.

Your Contribution describes how you want to make a difference by adding value to others. This means that 'Value' can also include items under the next heading, such as improving your energy resources by developing health priorities, or having priorities that focus on developing your financial resources, etc. The 'Others' includes your loved ones, clients, the organization where you work, or the world at large. After completing the Life Balance Self-Assessment in Chapter 5, list your current top 3 priorities:

1.   \-

2.   \-

3.   \-

Time (Describes your Inputs)

Time, includes your time (duh), effort and other resources invested in achieving the above results or making your contribution. You have a limited amount of time, energy and resources (financial or other) available to commit to achieving your desired outcomes. For better results you need to prioritize carefully and plan effectively, based on what is most important to you. After completing the Life Balance Self-Assessment in Chapter 5, map out how you would like to spend your typical 24 hour week day, based on the above top 3 priorities, using a blank page or daily view calendar or diary. Remember to include how many hours you are planning to sleep, eat, commute, work on personal projects, spend time with family, etc.

Use this activity to plan how to leverage your use of time on a daily basis to allow for optimal focus on your most important priorities. The next step is to expand this by doing the same thing on a weekly, monthly and yearly basis, in order to plan how you will spend your time, energy and resources, on weekends, vacation time and other important long term priorities.

It is also possible to combine certain activities to optimize your use of time to create more leverage. For example, you could listen to audio books during your daily commute to save time on reading in the evenings. This would enable you to spend more time looking after your health by going for a run, or building your relationship with your child by helping with their homework, cooking dinner with your partner, or whatever is matters most to you.

In the book we will unpack a 3-step framework, which involves the analysis of three key personal data sets for leveraging your productivity exponentially:

The 3-Step Framework:

1. Categorizing – A sorting activity for your Task List data to group related tasks into categories and create Your Segmented Task List (discussed in Chapter 2). This will enable you to work in a more structured way, as well as provide a foundation for prioritizing and focusing more effectively.

2. Optimizing – A planning activity for your Schedule data to optimize calendar activities and create Your Leveraged Schedule (discussed in Chapter 3). This will enable you to spend more time on high value activities that bring you the results you want.

3. Prioritizing – A self-assessment activity for your Personal Values data to prioritize your time allocation based on your personal values and create Your Filter of Focus (discussed in Chapter 5). This will enable you to focus on what is most important to you, as you go back to revisit and refine your categorizing and optimizing activities.

At the end of the last chapter of this book a further level of productivity is introduced, the Personal Best program, where you can discover how to start making a greater difference right now, and find true satisfaction in your work, regardless of your current role. Connect with me on LinkedIn to find out more.

linkedin.com/in/jacques-soine-56a3bb37

Part 1: Leverage - My Favorite Three Simple Productivity Tips for the Office

Chapter 1: Complete Workflow Mastery - Empty your Inbox

In the office environment email can be a major source of incoming demands on your time, from reading them to responding to the requests contained in them, they can easily lead to overwhelm. One of my colleagues was recently showing me something on his computer screen and switched to his email inbox to search for a related document. I happened to notice that he had over 2000 unread emails. I can't help wondering what important or urgent tasks may be hidden within all of those unread items, and how long it would take to work through all of them. I would struggle to sleep at night!

I use a simple workflow processing system to complete administrative tasks (like processing emails) efficiently. One of the best proven resources out there for the purpose of managing workflow is probably David Allen's *Getting Things Done*. Here is my take on of some of the key elements for managing workflow and email.

Tasks and information arrive in your inbox in the form of physical and electronic documents, emails, telephone calls, and a wide range of other messages and requests. Workflow can be simply mastered by using a 2-step sorting process for all incoming information. This sorting process should be viewed as a task on its own, separate from the other tasks that it identifies. You can then work on the other tasks after the sorting step has been completed.

1.   The first step is to sort everything according to three possible types: File, Action, or Delete. Filing is for any information you will need for future reference. Action is for any tasks to be completed. Delete is for anything that you do not need now or for future reference. It is also a good practice to review your subscriptions to

mailing lists and newsletters periodically. Our interests and needs change and if you don't take the time to unsubscribe from what is no longer useful, it can end up wasting a lot of time every day by clogging up your inbox. I recommend https://unroll.me/ for this purpose. It will help you to clean up your inbox by listing all of your email subscriptions and allow you to easily unsubscribe from whatever you don't want anymore.

The primary goal of the sorting step is to isolate all tasks requiring action to add to your To Do List or Tasks.

2.   The next step, after filing and deleting, is to sort all of the tasks that you have identified to be completed, according to three possible actions: Do, Defer, or Delegate. Do any quick tasks immediately to get them out of the way. Defer more complex or time consuming tasks, by adding them to your To Do List or Tasks in MS Outlook to work on later. Delegate everything that doesn't require your personal attention. Delegation is a very effective way of saving time for more important tasks, but only works if done

correctly. We will cover delegating in more detail later. Delegating is one of the key secrets to buying back time on an exponential level. For example, if you manage to successfully delegate a repeatable 1 hour weekly task in the correct way, you will have effectively saved 4 hours or a half day per month on an ongoing basis, but more on that in the next chapter.

For the quick tasks that can be completed immediately, you can save even more time by using templates or saved scripts for common email requests that you receive frequently. You can save these well thought out and carefully worded responses as different email signatures, or as email templates in your drafts folder, or just save them in an easily accessible document to select when required. So, instead of typing out your response to the same request a few times every day, just select the relevant signature template, or copy and paste.

Managing workflow using this 2-step process separates the processing or sorting of incoming information, from working on completing the actual tasks themselves. Processing becomes a separate initial task, and this step radically improves productivity results. It allows you to work on administrative tasks in a more structured and pro-active way, rather than jumping from one unrelated task to another in a reactive way as you work through your inbox or respond to incoming requests. You can also use this approach to blast through your entire email inbox in one sitting or in batches at regular intervals during the day. You don't work on the incoming tasks contained in the emails when you do this – you just focus on the primary task of sorting them. In this way you can clear your entire email inbox. Yes, it is possible! Knowing that reference items have been filed in the relevant folders, all the junk mail and spam has been deleted and anything requiring action has been recorded on your To Do List or in your Tasks. Create different folders for related emails that you need keep. You can also insert emails into the task information in MS Outlook so that when you open a task to work on it, the relevant emails are immediately accessible there without having to search for them (they remain there, even if you delete the original email from your inbox). I realize that there are other much cooler products out there besides MS Office, it just happens to be my primary frame of reference, because it is used in the organizations where I work. You can apply the principles to the platforms you are using to manage tasks and email. Using an email inbox as a makeshift To Do List is one of the most inefficient ways to manage tasks! Surprisingly I have found that many people still do this, marking emails as 'unread', as a reminder to go back to them later. This results in an informal task list in your inbox that consists of 'unread' emails in random order that you have to search through when you are ready to do the work. The dangers of working in this way are obvious. You end up wasting time searching for things, risk missing deadlines, and set yourself up to work through items in a reactive way that lacks focus. Your inbox will probably never be completely empty, but you can avoid leaving emails there for more than 48 hours.

The first prize when it comes to managing email is usually to have the entire function outsourced to an assistant or team member, provided your role allows for this option. There are also a number of very professional Virtual Assistant services available online, which are particularly useful to independent small business owners. However, for the purpose of this section, I am assuming that these options are not currently applicable to your role, or that your role includes email management for others.

Now that you've read the section on emptying your inbox, take a few minutes to answer the following questions:

1. How can this help me to be more productive?

2. How can this help me to feel less stressed?

3. How can this help me to add more value?

4. What action do I need to take to apply this in my job immediately?

Summary Notes

1. Sort incoming information using the two step process to empty your inbox daily

2. Separate the sorting task from the other tasks

3. Setup a simple Task List to manage your work

4. Don't use your email inbox as a To Do List!

5. Take a few minutes to unsubscribe from mailing lists that are no longer useful

6. Create templates or scripts to save time responding to common email requests that you receive frequently

Chapter 2: One Structured List - The Foundation for Prioritizing

This is a really simple one, have one list of everything to do. Stop searching for things, forgetting things, and worrying about things. The list can be electronic or paper-based, but preferably electronic and integrated into your email and calendar. If you use MS Outlook for email, it is quite convenient to use the Tasks functionality. The most important principle is that everything is in one place. Don't have notes and lists of things to do scattered about on sticky notes, on your phone, in your diary or calendar, emails marked as unread in your inbox, or worst of all, in your head. If you allow this to happen, you could lose track of deadlines, feel overwhelmed, forget something important, and waste a lot of time searching for things. It will also make the next two vital list-practices of categorizing and prioritizing tasks, close to impossible to implement. So, have one list of things to do.

Structure your list by categorizing or grouping related tasks together. A segmented list helps you to work in a structured way for increased focus and efficiency. You can schedule time to work on specific task categories, for example: preparing reports, making travel bookings, or returning phone calls. MS Outlook also allows you to create and assign categories to your tasks and sort your list accordingly. The worst thing about an unstructured list is that you end up jumping from one unrelated task to another, and prioritizing becomes a challenge. If you want to work on reports, all of the reports that you need to prepare at any given time can be found in the Reports category in your task list. You can also create recurring tasks, such as preparing monthly or weekly reports.

Prioritize your list categories according to what is most important. Prioritizing effectively is the most powerful way to increase productivity, by spending more time on the things that matter most to you and your results. There are a number of different frames of reference for prioritizing, examples include: your role description, your key performance indicators or appraisal criteria, your manager's priorities, organizational objectives, your personal values and your business objectives. The important thing is to understand, schedule, communicate and protect your priorities. This also means learning when and how to say 'no' to others' demands on your time, and to delegate tasks that don't require your personal attention.

The Eisenhower Matrix is a priority matrix ascribed to the 34th president of the USA that ranks tasks according to their urgency and importance. The tasks with highest value usually fall into the category of important, but not urgent. These include tasks such as planning, clarification of values, relaxation, exercise, and building relationships. Increased focus on these 'quality tasks' will also keep you from constantly ending up in crisis mode, having to deal primarily with urgent tasks most of the time.

The Pareto Principle is another useful way of identifying high-value tasks, also known as the 80–20 Rule. This principle suggests that in general, roughly 80% of our results come from 20% of our actions. The principle is named after the Italian economist Vilfredo Pareto, who showed that approximately 80% of the land in Italy was owned by 20% of the population in 1896. According to Wikipedia, he developed the principle by observing that 20% of the pea pods in his garden contained 80% of the peas. Identify which of your tasks fall under the 20% that delivers 80% of your results, and focus more on these. Gain clarity on the few activities that bring you the highest returns, and then arrange your life around making sure that you get those activities done consistently. Simple, but extremely powerful! Can you identify what your top 20%, highest value tasks are?

Some also recommend extracting a daily shortlist of 3-5 things to do for the day each morning. These items are your list of non-negotiable tasks to be completed regardless of what else happens in your day.

You can also add a delegation category to your list for everything that others can do, and use it for follow-up. You can assign tasks in MS Outlook and create a separate category for them. Learn to delegate any 'busy work' that doesn't require your personal attention, especially repeatable tasks. This will facilitate the ongoing buy-back of time and provide an opportunity for your leadership development.

Delegating for maximum productivity

For delegation to be effective, you need to pay careful attention to who you delegate to, what you delegate, when to delegate, and how you delegate. Otherwise you will end up feeling like most people do, believing that if you want something done properly, you have to do it yourself. Remember that when you delegate, you assign authority and responsibility to someone else to complete the task, but you remain accountable for the result. Effective delegation requires a substantial time investment upfront, but the exponential returns going forward cannot be ignored. I once delegated an entire accounting process to an employee who was eager to develop. Not only did it free up two days of my time every month to use for more high value tasks, but it gave me an opportunity to mentor someone. That employee later went on to greater achievements in an accounting role, and it was wonderful to watch her progress.

For example, if you take one repeatable task: Preparing a weekly report (60 minutes). Invest two hours to transfer the skill, and two one-hour follow up sessions for feedback and coaching to competence, that's a four hour time investment. Thereafter you will get back 60 minutes per week, or four hours per month. That's an extra working week in your year! Remember that it will take you one month to recover your initial four hour investment. Thereafter you get an exponential time refund, as someone else puts in the time to produce the report for you. You now get to decide how you will spend the extra time in a way that maximizes your return, by using it for a high value, top priority task or activity. However, you may not like the idea of delegating, and I realize that some things cannot be delegated, but usually there is at least something on your list that doesn't require your personal attention and can be delegated.

Delegation is about making the best use of your time. Ask the question: am I the only person who can do this, or can I make better use of my time? When we delegate, we assign authority and responsibility to another, while remaining accountable for the result. It can be very challenging to delegate if you're not used to it. Letting go and handing over responsibility for something that you will remain accountable for is not easy. Learning how to teach or mentor someone to master a new skill might not be something that you've done before. Do you believe that getting something done properly means having to do it yourself? This is usually the result having asked somebody to do something for you in the past, and being let down. Firstly, this is not delegating. Secondly, you need to realize that delegating takes a significant time commitment initially, but the future gains are well worth the effort.

I recommend the following 5-step process for delegating tasks, after an agreement has been reached with the person that you are delegating to:

1. Prepare to delegate. Decide beforehand how you will share the necessary

information, transfer the skills required, and monitor progress.

2. Explain the task in detail and encourage questions. Also explain the value of the task and how it fits into the bigger picture.

3. Demonstrate or show them how to do the task.

4. Give them an opportunity to explain their understanding of task and observe them doing it.

5. Provide constructive feedback and coach them to competence.

Finding the time to do this may seem like an impossible task, but once you understand the enormous potential value locked inside of the delegation process, you will find ways to make it happen more often.

Create a "Not-To-Do List"

Identify and eliminate as much "clutter" as possible from your life and work environment. This can include a messy and cluttered desk, but also any other distractions, escape activities, and bad or wasteful habits.

Practice Saying 'No'

Some of us also have a tendency to say 'yes' to everyone and find it difficult or uncomfortable to say 'no'. You cannot please everyone. Saying 'no' does not have to feel rude and unhelpful, it should be about understanding, affirming, protecting, and communicating your priorities to others. Be vigilant about what gets onto your list!

Summary Notes

1. Have one list

2. Categorize your list

3. Prioritize your list

4. Extract a daily short list

5. Make a delegation list and learn to delegate

6. Create a Not-To-Do List

7. Practice saying 'no' and be vigilant about what gets onto your list

Chapter 3: Planning for Action – Leverage your Schedule

Benjamin Franklin said, "If you fail to plan, you are planning to fail." The importance of setting aside regular time for various kinds of planning to increase productivity cannot be over-emphasized. At the very least, set aside 15 minutes every morning to make your short list for the day. Know at the start of every day where you are going to focus your energy. Stop functioning in crisis mode and become value, quality and priority oriented. Daily planning will also help you to maintain some big-picture perspective for better focus, before you step into all the distractions and urgency of a busy day. Use your Calendar to plan daily, weekly, monthly and annually. Steven Covey suggested that rather than prioritizing what's on our schedule, we should schedule our priorities. This means that the high value priorities that you identify need to be scheduled. Otherwise they will be left to chance, if you remember, or if you have enough time left after dealing with all the other urgent items. Simply, treat priorities accordingly and include them in your action plans, to make sure they get done! If you don't have a proactive plan for what you want to do, you will end up reacting to everything else that crosses your path, without the necessary awareness or consciousness about the bigger picture, to stay on track towards your goals.

Typically we use Calendars for scheduling routine activities, meetings, appointments, time off, business travel, and important events.

Project Plans are used for multi-step tasks. You can also create comprehensive checklists or templates for planning simple recurring projects like events.

You can create Action Plans to achieve goals linked to your priorities and values, such as an Exercise Plan, a Nutrition Plan, or a Study Timetable.

It is helpful to break goals down into smaller milestones and more manageable step-by-step tasks that can be scheduled. In this way you will have practical steps to take on a daily basis that will lead you closer to achieving your desired result. Proper planning takes time and also needs to be scheduled. The fact that it takes time to plan, when you are already under pressure to complete urgent tasks, is the reason most people don't bother to plan on a regular basis. However, once you understand and appreciate the benefits of doing this, there is no valid excuse. Planning is one of the best ways to avoid ending up with too many urgent tasks in the first place.

Starting with a 15 minute daily action planning session in the morning, will ensure that you know where you are going to focus your energy at the start of each day. This is how we implement what we have prioritized, because prioritizing without implementing is a waste of time.

You can leverage your use of time by simply taking an ordinary calendar page out of your schedule for one day, and use it to map out your current use of time. Enter your activities from the time you wake up until the time you go to sleep. Include things like how long you take to get ready in the morning, your travel time to and from work, work time activities, breaks, exercise activities, meals, family time, hobbies, and anything else included in your normal daily routine. Then evaluate the resulting picture:

1. How many hours do you typically sleep?

2. How much time do you spend travelling to and from work?

3. Consider time spent and frequency of meals and exercise.

4. How much time is devoted to your most important relationships?

5. How many hours do you spend working, relaxing, etc.?

Now think about potential ways to improve or optimize your use of time. Be as critical and creative as possible. It is natural to resist change and find excuses as to why a new idea won't work, so be aware of this and take action accordingly. Be guided by your priorities, and come back to this activity again, after you have completed the next 2 chapters to find even more efficiencies.

You can improve your use of time by moving, changing, reducing, increasing, combining, removing, or adding activities to your schedule. So approach the activity with these strategies in mind. The idea is to find leverage – think about the example I shared in the Introduction about how I exchanged two draining hours of time in the traffic, for two extra quiet hours at my desk on weekdays. Don't be afraid to try out a new idea a few times before deciding on what works best for you. There is no pressure to find perfect solutions on the first attempt. It is a personal growth process – the important thing is to be open to doing things differently to find the scenario that works best for you.

Summary Notes

1. Planning is essential to improving productivity

2. Set aside 15 minutes every morning to plan your day

3. Leverage your daily schedule to optimize your use of time

4. Focus on quality and high value priorities

5. Use planning to achieve your goals, with resources like Task Lists, Calendars, Project Plans, and Action Plans.

To encourage the application of everything we have covered in these first 3 chapters, set aside a few minutes to answer the following questions. I recommend that you actually write something down.

1. What can I start doing?

2. What can I do more of?

3. What can I stop doing?

4. What can I do less of?

5. What can I delegate?

6. What can I do differently in terms of:

a. Workflow

b. Lists

c. Planning

If you decide to choose even just one or two things out of these first three chapters to increase your productivity and save time every day, it will already have a significant impact on your results.

If you manage to save 30 minutes a day, that's 10 hours per month, which is equivalent to more than a full working day to yourself. You can use that time to get more of the things that are most important to your results done. This excludes the immeasurable value of potentially having less stress, more clarity of purpose, better health, a greater sense of achievement, peace, enjoyment, and satisfaction in your life. Here are a few examples to get you thinking:

1.   Stop using your inbox as a To Do List: potential gain, immeasurable. The resulting efficiencies from making this change can be truly staggering, depending on the nature of your work.

2.   Delegate one repeatable task: potential gain, dependent on the task duration and frequency, as well as the time required to transfer the skill effectively.

3.   Identify one non-negotiable high value task per day or week (three client calls, 30 minutes at gym, date night, or family dinner)

4.   Get eight hours of sleep every night by setting two alarms, one to wake up and one to go to sleep.

5.   Start an exercise routine (recruit an accountability partner)

6.   Stop using social media or browsing news sites during certain periods of your day

7.   Plan your entire week every Friday, or Sunday

8.   Set aside 15 minutes every morning to plan your day and get focused

9. Take one of your major personal goals and break it down into a few smaller steps that can be scheduled and achieved over time.

10. Or do all of the above and completely transform your productivity!

Part 2: Productivity with Purpose

Chapter 4: New Routines to Transform Old Habits - A Process

Leadership expert John Maxwell said "you'll never change your life until you change something you do daily. The secret of your success is found in your daily routine." In the same way, the secret behind our lack of success in certain areas of life can also be attributed to our daily habits. The habitual behaviors that are producing the results in your life at the moment are the same ones that will keep you from achieving any significant change or progress in future.

 A huge part of improving productivity is linked to change, replacing unhelpful habits with better ones. A useful way to create a new habit is to establish a new routine or daily ritual, which over time will become as natural as a habit. While habits drive our behavior on a subconscious level, engaging in a new routine is very much a conscious choice and can be quite challenging at first. You need to be clear on the purpose and goal of the routine and constantly affirm and assimilate it daily until it becomes part of your new reality. Various studies have shown that it takes consistency and daily repetition over a period of approximately 30 to 45 days to establish a new habit. It is a process, not a quick fix. Remember when you first learnt to drive a car? There was so much to concentrate on all at the same time: checking mirrors, indicating, changing gears, braking, etc. I've watched my own kids struggle with this when they first started out, but after months of practice they were all eventually able to pass the test. If you've been driving a car for a few years, you will realize that it has become completely natural to you, and requires far less conscious effort than it did in the beginning. It is the same with forming a new health habit, like getting up 30 minutes earlier to go for a run. You just have to want it as much as you wanted to drive that car when you were a teenager. If you persevere, you will find that after a few months, you will be in the habit of getting up early to go for a run. When you are on vacation, or travelling for business, you will be able to feel that your normal routine has been interrupted. You will have established a new habit, one that supports your health and success.

Here are three common habits that destroy productivity and increase stress, together with some suggested routines to transform your results going forward. They may not all apply to your personal situation, but you can apply the principles to your own challenges.

1.   The morning rush habit: The morning rush is a collection of behaviors that sabotage your productivity before you even get your day started. If you are inclined to snooze the alarm, skip breakfast, stop for fuel, drop the kids off late at school, deal with crises on your phone before getting to work, dive into urgent emails, or rush off to meetings - you are probably a victim of this habit. It is the, 'I don't know where I'm going and don't have time to check, I'm just trying to keep my head above water' habit. It has poorly developed focus, very little planning, a lack of

value-based priorities, and consequently hardly any purpose directed activity. You will stay very busy, but will hardly be productive, often feeling the pressure of having more things to do than time available to do them in. This is a stressful, unfulfilling, and unsustainable habit.

Recommendation: learn to implement a Daily Start-up Routine. This also happens to be a key habit of most top performers out there. It involves establishing a new way to start the day, by taking time out to focus on what matters most, and setting the tone for an awesome day. It involves making the necessary adjustments to your current lifestyle (like going to bed earlier at night, so that you can get up earlier in the morning), to create that precious extra 20 minutes needed to start off on the right foot. This may sound impossible at first, but through proper planning and commitment it is possible to set up new routines, create the life-balance and focus you want, and get out of stressful habits like the morning rush. The Daily Start-up Routine is about taking some quality time every morning to do things like:

a.   Prioritize your task list

b.   Plan your schedule

c.   Clarify your values

d.   Affirm your goals

e.   Be inspired

f.   Exercise

g.   Read

h.   Pray

The Daily Start-up Routine should become a habit of personal development and discipline, which supports planned goal-directed activity, and is a preventive approach to dealing with stress. In the same way that your body needs nutrition daily, your mind also needs daily input to sustain your motivation levels and a positive outlook. A daily start-up routine is also an ideal way to facilitate the process of personal growth.

2.   The running on empty habit: Running on empty is characterized by beliefs like, I don't have time for exercise, I can't afford gym, I get home too late to cook, I'll settle for fast food convenience, I'm going to watch one more episode, I just want to get past the next level, I need a cup of coffee, or I'm just too tired. It has so many excuses, a lack of discipline, poor nutrition, low energy, and a permanent feeling that you deserve a break. You feel like you're burning the candle at both ends and have nothing left for exercise or healthy food choices. You escape into hours of binge-watching, comfort food, socializing, drinking, or other entertainment habits to soothe your stress. Unfortunately your efforts only serve to compound your problem with unwanted weight gain, sleep deprivation, lethargy, and a dangerous downward spiral of deteriorating health and energy levels.

Recommendation: Learn to implement a Daily Health and Fitness Routine. This also happens to be a key habit of high-energy professionals. It may seem counter-intuitive to use up more energy exercising when you already feel exhausted, but experience has taught me that a healthier, fitter body soon starts an upward spiral of increased energy and improved concentration, more restful sleep patterns, and an inspired sense of wellbeing. The practice of pouring sugar and caffeine into a fatigued body only provides a short-term solution, while creating a bigger long-term problem. It is difficult to change habits at first and most of us have tried and failed at least once before. Implement a daily start-up routine to feed your motivation to get through the painful start, and on to conquering stressful habits like running on empty, forever.

The Daily Health and Fitness Routine, is about making your health a high value priority and setting up structures to support a successful and sustainable transformation:

a.   Start an exercise plan (there is so much information available online)

b.   Design an eating plan (including daily menus, shopping lists, and checklists)

c.   Get to sleep by 10pm on weeknights

d.   Get a personal trainer or an accountability partner

e.   Sign up for a dance, martial arts, social soccer, or yoga class

f.   Or start using those fitness DVDs or exercise equipment that you already purchased and now neglect

The Daily Health and Fitness Routine will boost your energy and effectiveness under pressure, lower your stress levels and help you to become more productive and confident.

Personal Trainers are great if you can afford them, but making a commitment to a friend or family member to get some regular exercise together, can also be an effective solution, provided there is accountability. For me, designing an eating plan is partly about making sure that you eat what your body needs and avoid what is harmful, but it's more about knowing what you're going to eat and where to get it, before you feel hungry. This will prevent you from falling back on the fast food drive-through whenever you're running late or there isn't time to pack lunch. Be disciplined and use menus with corresponding shopping lists to ensure you have what you need when you need it. If you don't like cooking, there are many services available offering healthy home-cooked meal portions. You can freeze them, or have fresh daily delivery to your home or office. This can also save you money every month in the process. I'm not talking about store-bought microwave meals. They are usually both expensive and unhealthy. If you're not ready to take such big steps immediately, you can focus on changing one bad habit at a time, such as cutting out sugary carbonated drinks, or starting your day with a healthy breakfast. Getting enough sleep is mostly about discipline. We set alarms to wake up in the morning, but are probably more in need of one to remind us that it's time for bed. Make sure that you get eight hours of sleep every night. You will be amazed at the results. Bedtime is dependent on what time you have to be up in the morning. For most of us that means going to sleep no later than 10pm during the week. Try not to see this as 'giving up on the day', but rather as 'preparing for another day of excellent results'.

3.   The stress commute habit: The stress commute is characterized by traffic frustration, transport delays, waiting in queues, wasted hours, arriving late and exhausted. It has no benefit besides getting you to your destination, there is no enjoyment or fulfillment, it's just 'in-between time'. At the very least, you experience boredom and impatience. The worst case scenarios produce stress, anxiety, anger, high blood pressure, and possibly even a helpless sense of being trapped with 'no other choice'. These are the hours simply wasted while waiting to arrive at home or at work.

 A helpful solution is to replace this habit, with a productive Daily Travel Routine. Whether you drive yourself to work, or use public transport, there are many ways to make this time count for more than just a wait. Decide to be productive during these hours of your day and you will be amazed at the results:

a.   Invest in your personal development or education

b.   Relax and enjoy some energizing leisure time

c.   Listen to an audio book or your favorite music playlist

d.   Combine your Daily Travel Routine with your Health and Fitness Routine

You can actually look forward to your Daily Travel Routine, if it's all about your time to be inspired, learn something new, relax or be entertained. You will be far less focused on any stressful aspects of your trip. It may feel strange in the beginning, if you haven't done it before, but you will soon find yourself in a new comfort zone.

If you have your book, audiobook or music playlist with you on your device of choice, you can create your own world of enjoyment, listening to or reading material that is inspirational, educational, entertaining, or relaxing. You can read or listen to your favorite comedian, radio talk show, music playlist, motivational coach, or educational program.

Combining this routine with your Health and Fitness goals only applies if your logistics make it practical, but some are able to walk or cycle to work. You could attend a gym that is located near to where you work and travel there early, straight after waking up. You will miss peak traffic congestion, save enormously on travel time and fuel, and get your exercise and a shower done there before work.

Think about appropriate routines for these other important areas in your life.

4.   True Rest, Recreation, and Relaxation: During work time it is helpful to space your work time productivity blocks with short rest breaks to recharge your energy and concentration levels. A balanced lifestyle will also include leisure activities that you enjoy outside of the work environment during your personal time, like vacations, weekends, evenings, and public holidays. This can include family time, hobbies, interests, socializing, travel, sport, etc. There is more to life than work. If you don't create balance in your life, you risk serious consequences to your health and happiness. This

can also eventually impact directly on your work performance too. What are your favorite leisure-time activities? How much time do you spend on these activities? How does this make you feel? Do you take any regular breaks during your working day to re-charge energy and concentration levels? If not, have you ever noticed a drop in your productivity at certain times of the day? Create an action plan to address any development areas identified by answering these questions.

5.   Important Relationships: It is helpful to set up planned time and activities for the important relationships in your life. If we neglect our relationships with our significant others, spouses, children, family, friends, and colleagues, we risk far more than just missing a deadline at work. Who are the most important people in your life? Do you spend as much time with them as you would like to? What are some of the ultimate consequences of neglecting relationships? Think of three ways you could plan time and activities for important relationships in your life.

You can apply this kind of thinking to every area of your life.

Summary Notes

1. Replace old negative habits with new positive routines

2. Practice and persevere for at least 30-45 days to assimilate the new behavior

3. The Daily Start-up Routine

4. The Daily Fitness Routine

5. The Daily Travel Routine

6. True Rest, Recreation, and Relaxation

7. Important Relationships

Chapter 5: Your Filter of Focus - The Next Level

Emotional Intelligence and Personal Productivity are closely linked. Daniel Goleman, considered by many to be the leading authority on EI theory, highlights Self-awareness and Self-management as two key personal development areas. We've already established that everyone has the same amount of time available each day. The challenge is to manage what and how we do what we do with our time. This clearly falls into the Self-management category. The previous chapters look primarily at how to do things more efficiently and effectively, which can be of great value, but if you can learn to better leverage what you do with your time, you will be able to decrease your stress and increase your productivity exponentially. The challenge is that when we start considering the what, it usually also ends up leading to the much deeper question of why. These are the deeper questions about what motivates us in life, our vision for the future, our values, our personal mission, and our sense of purpose that drives our decisions and actions on a daily basis. When we start to think and reflect at this level, we increase our self-awareness and become more mindful of what our true priorities are. After all, we don't just want to get a whole bunch of stuff done. Most of us would like to do our best work, make a difference, be recognized for our contribution, experience love and trust in relationships, and leave a legacy. Developing self-awareness at this level requires some conscious effort. So it's helpful to engage in a few activities to facilitate the process.

I have included the Life Balance Self-assessment here for you, because it can be a good place to start. It will get you thinking about your life beyond the level of just getting more things done at work.

When you have completed the exercise, you will have a Filter of Focus that you can apply to chapters 2 and 3 of this book. Use the application of your personal values to prioritizing your task list, and leveraging your schedule.

Life Balance Self-Assessment

In the table below, first fill in the different areas of your life from A to J at the top (for example: Health, Career, Spouse, Family, Recreation, Education, Social, Community, Spiritual, Financial, etc.). Then rate each of them on a scale of 1 to 10 in terms of how satisfied you are with your current progress in each area (10 being the highest level of satisfaction and 1 being the lowest) by placing an 'x' in the relevant block under each heading from A to J. Once you have rated all of them, prioritize them from 1 to 10 using the Priority Scale along the bottom of the table (1 being the highest priority and 10 being the lowest). How do your satisfaction ratings compare with your priority scale? What rating did your top priority get on the scale of 1 to 10 in terms of your current satisfaction level in that area?

Life Graph Rating	A	B	C	D	E	F	G	H	I	J
10										
9										
8										
7										
6										
5										
4										
3										
2										
1										
Priority Scale (1-10)										

Consider the following questions:

1.   What has this exercise revealed about your life at the moment?

2.   Which areas are you doing relatively well in?

3.   Which areas are you not doing relatively well in?

4.   Which areas of your life have been neglected and how important are they to you?

5.   What are your most important priorities and how did you rate them?

6.   What are the most important changes you would like to make when you look at your life graph?

7.   List 3 things you need to do to improve the current situation:

a.

b.

c.

The Life Balance Self-Assessment is designed to improve self-awareness, help clarify your values, and develop your sense of what is most important to you, so that your priorities rapidly begin to crystalize. You should easily see what you need to be spending more of your time on to start living the life you want. The goal is to add more value for yourself, your significant relationships, and in your work. We have covered the Priority Matrix, the Pareto Principle, and the power of new routines to transform old habits. But when your priorities are guided by your core values and your ultimate sense of what matters most in life, you will start to experience a new level of productivity.

If you are interested in exploring this topic further, connect with me on LinkedIn and enquire about the Personal Best program, "start making a difference right now, and find true satisfaction in your work, regardless of your current role."

linkedin.com/in/jacques-soine-56a3bb37.

Author

Jacques is currently employed as a Management Accountant at a US-funded NPO in Cape Town, South Africa. With 20+ years of Finance and Business Management experience through both formal employment in the packaging industry, and independent entrepreneurship in the corporate training field. He enjoys roles that provide the opportunity to make a difference by adding measurable value.

linkedin.com/in/jacques-soine-56a3bb37